What Is the World Series?

by Gail Herman

illustrated by David Grayson Kenyon

Penguin Workshop

For my father, who cheered on the Miracle Mets with me—GH

PENGUIN WORKSHOP
An Imprint of Penguin Random House LLC, New York

Published by Penguin Workshop, an imprint of Penguin Random House LLC, New York.
PENGUIN and PENGUIN WORKSHOP are trademarks of Penguin Books Ltd.
WHO HQ & Design is a registered trademark of Penguin Random House LLC.
Printed in the USA.

Visit us online at www.penguinrandomhouse.com.

Library of Congress Control Number: 2015942834

ISBN 9780448484068 15 14

Contents

BASE BALL
O.M.O
EMERSON

What Is the World Series?

It was October 1, 1903, and the first World Series game was about to begin. Hours before the game, thousands of fans poured into the Huntington Avenue Baseball Grounds in Boston. They came by foot, by horse and buggy, and by trolley car.

By 2:00 p.m., all nine thousand seats were taken. Seven thousand more fans filed in, sitting on fences and standing behind ropes around the outfield. For this game, admission was double the usual cost: fifty cents for standing room and bleacher seats. One dollar for grandstand seats.

Businessmen, students, factory workers. The rich and the poor. Fans from all backgrounds came—with one exception. African Americans were not welcome in the stands or on the field.

(In fact, there would be no black players in Major League Baseball until 1947.)

At 3:00 p.m., an announcer shouted out the lineup through a megaphone. The game pitted the Boston Americans against the Pittsburgh Pirates.

In the first inning, Honus Wagner brought one of his Pirates teammates home with a line-drive single. It was the very first run scored in the very first World Series.

Every October, the temperature drops. Leaves fall. Excitement fills the air for baseball fans. It's time for the World Series—a once-a-year contest between the best of the Major Leagues—to name a championship team.

But the World Series is more than a competition. It's an event with a capital *E*. During those autumn days, it captures the attention of the entire United States. Presidents throw out first pitches. Popular singers belt out the national anthem. In wartime, in peacetime, in good times and bad, the World Series celebrates a game that has become so popular, it is known as the national pastime.

CHAPTER 1
In the Beginning

Since the mid-1800s, the game of baseball has been played pretty much the way we know it today. However, until 1869, there were no professional teams with paid players. The Cincinnati Red Stockings were the first pro team. Others followed, and in time the teams joined leagues, which had rules, schedules, and player contracts.

Teams traveled from city to city by railroad. Reporters went, too. They wrote up stories on new machines called typewriters. And they sent news by telegraph.

Newspapers started "sports pages," drumming up interest in the game. Fans started following teams.

By the late 1800s, there were two major leagues, the National League of Professional Baseball Clubs and its rival, the American Association of Baseball Clubs. Teams had names like the Boston Beaneaters, the Brooklyn Bridegrooms, and the Chicago Orphans. Some teams faded away. Some changed their names. But others, like the Giants and the Athletics, are still going strong.

Each league awarded its top team a pennant. In 1882, the AA's Cincinnati Reds challenged the

NL's Chicago White Stockings to postseason games. Some consider this to be the first true World Series. The teams tied, winning two games apiece. But the series was so successful, the leagues agreed to continue playing postseason games every year.

But what would these games be called? In 1884, they were advertised as "the championship of the United States." That soon changed to the "World's Championship Series" and then just the World Series.

The AA folded in 1891, and the new American League took its place. The following year, the Pittsburgh Pirates looked to be the NL pennant winner. Owner Barney Dreyfuss wrote to Henry Killilea, owner of the Boston Americans, the top team in the AL.

“The time has come for the National League and the American League to organize a World Series.” So the owners met. They agreed on dates and rules. They shook hands. It wasn’t official. But the modern World Series was born.

Major League Teams in 1903

National League

Boston Beaneaters (Renamed the Boston Braves. Moved to Milwaukee in 1953, Atlanta in 1966)

Brooklyn Superbas (Renamed the Robins, then the Brooklyn Dodgers. Moved to Los Angeles in 1958)

Chicago Cubs

Cincinnati Reds

New York Giants (Moved to San Francisco in 1958)

Philadelphia Phillies

Pittsburgh Pirates

St. Louis Cardinals

1903 Boston Beaneaters

American League

Boston Americans (Also called the Pilgrims, renamed the Boston Red Sox)

Chicago White Sox

Cleveland Naps (Named for star second baseman Napoleon "Nap" Lajoie. Renamed the Cleveland Indians)

Detroit Tigers

New York Highlanders (Renamed the New York Yankees)

Philadelphia Athletics (Moved to Oakland, California, in 1968)

St. Louis Browns (Moved to Baltimore in 1954. Renamed the Baltimore Orioles)

Washington Senators (Moved to Minnesota in 1961. Renamed the Minnesota Twins)

1903 St. Louis Browns

CHAPTER 2
1900s: The World Series Takes Off

Where would baseball be without fans?

In the 1903 contest between the Pirates and the Americans, the fourth game of the World Series moved from Boston to Pittsburgh. Two hundred loyal Boston fans followed their team to Pennsylvania. These so-called "Royal Rooters" were the first members of what is now known as Red Sox Nation. Their team was down two games to one. But they had faith. And faith has always been an important part of baseball.

At Exposition Park in Pittsburgh, black clouds of smoke often billowed from nearby steel factories. That day, the sky was overcast, the field muddy. After eight innings, the Pirates were ahead 5–1. Famous slugger Honus Wagner had singled three times.

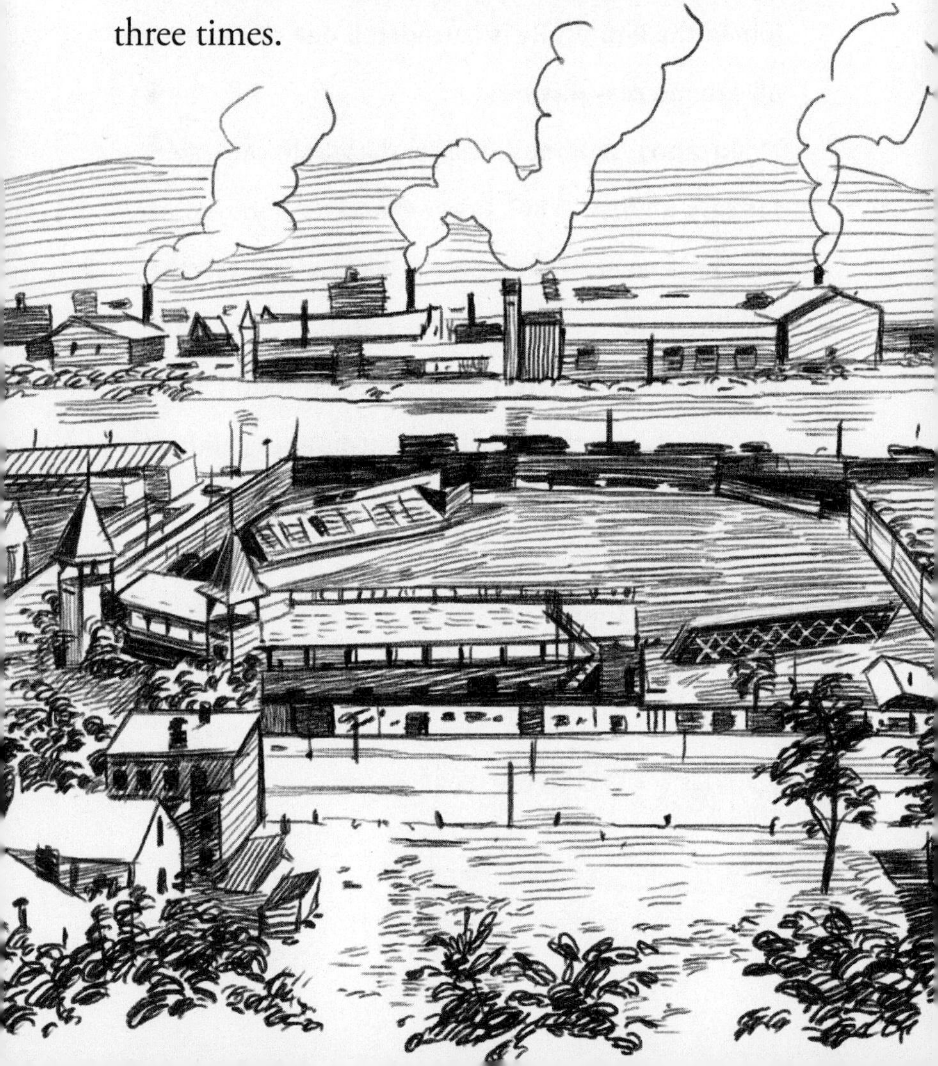

Honus Wagner (1874–1955)

Born in Pittsburgh, Honus Wagner left school at twelve to work in the coal mines, then he later joined the Pirates. He is considered one of the best all-around players ever.

In 2007, a Honus Wagner baseball card sold for $2.8 million. Why? Fewer than two hundred of the cards were printed before Wagner insisted the company stop production. The baseball cards were packaged with cigarettes, and Wagner didn't want to encourage children to smoke.

But something happened. The Royal Rooters began to sing. And in the top of the ninth, their ball club rallied with three runs.

It wasn't enough. But the Rooters kept singing. During game five, with Boston pitcher Cy Young on the mound, they changed the words to the hit song "Tessie." Instead of singing, "Tessie, you make me feel so badly," they sang, "Honus, why do you hit so badly?"

“You could hardly play ball they were singing so loud,” Pirate Tommy Leach recalled. The final play of that game—Young striking out Wagner.

"And before we knew what happened, we'd lost the World Series," Leach continued.

The Boston Americans won the first World Series. It was a best-of-nine contest. When the Series became official, the rules changed to best of seven—the same number there has been ever since. The only time a nine-game format was tried again was from 1919 to 1921.

World Series Winners

1903: Boston Americans over Pittsburgh Pirates

1904: No World Series (Top NL team, the New York Giants, refused to play.)

1905: New York Giants over Philadelphia Athletics (Giants pitching great Christy Mathewson had three shutouts in five days.)

1906: Chicago White Sox over Chicago Cubs

1907: Chicago Cubs over Detroit Tigers

1908: Chicago Cubs over Detroit Tigers

1909: Pittsburgh Pirates over Detroit Tigers

CHAPTER 3
1910s: Scandal!

By now, pro baseball was part of American life. Families went to games together. Some drove there in their new family cars, usually Ford Model Ts.

It was a thrilling time for Boston fans. Their team, now called the Red Sox, won the World Series in 1912, 1915, 1916, and 1918, with legendary player Babe Ruth leading the charge.

1918 Boston Red Sox

In Europe, World War I had been raging since 1914. Days before the 1917 season, the United States joined England and France against the Central Powers. The US government said men had to "work or fight" to support the war effort. That included baseball players.

By 1918, many players were serving in the military, including Tiger star hitter Ty Cobb and Christy Mathewson, the Giants ace pitcher.

The baseball season was cut short. The World Series was held in early September, and the Red Sox faced off against the Chicago Cubs. For the first time ever, "The Star-Spangled Banner" played at the Series.

Christy Mathewson and Ty Cobb

Babe Ruth pitched twenty-nine straight hitless innings, over two World Series, and helped the Red Sox to a 1918 Series victory. That was the Babe's last season with Boston. His contract was then sold to the Yankees. The Sox would never be the same. In fact, many fans thought the trade was the reason for what they considered a "curse." Without the Bambino, the Sox were not to win a Series for eighty years.

Watching the World Series

Before radio and TV, fans flocked to theaters to "watch" the Series games. An announcer read play-by-plays from telegraph messages, and actors portrayed the players onstage.

In time, electric scoreboards were invented. Placed in public spaces, like billboards, they stood as high as ten feet tall. Blinking lights showed ball movement. Some systems even added mechanical "dummy" players that moved around a baseball diamond stage. For the 1911 World Series, more New York fans (seventy thousand!) watched a board in Times Square than actually went to the games a few miles away.

After the war ended in 1918, baseball was back to business as usual. In 1919, the Chicago White Sox faced the Cincinnati Reds.

Everybody was sure the White Sox would win. Their players were the best. Pitching great Eddie Cicotte led the AL in wins. And "Shoeless" Joe Jackson, their star slugger, was an idol to millions. He was considered the greatest natural hitter ever.

Cincinnati hosted the first two games. Redland Park was packed. People watched from apartments overlooking the field. Fans crowded onto nearby roofs. Boys climbed telegraph poles. Chicago lost the first game in a 9–1 rout. They lost the second one, too. Cincinnati fans were thrilled, but surprised.

What is going on? they wondered. Nobody who followed baseball could believe it. Expert fielders were making errors! Pitching ace Eddie Cicotte couldn't throw strikes. Neither could Lefty Williams.

The teams took the overnight train to Chicago for the next game the following afternoon. Back then, parks didn't have lights. Games were always during the day.

Amazingly, the White Sox lost one of their first two home games. Now they were down three games to one.

For game five, Williams was back on the mound and stronger. But then in the top of the sixth inning, the White Sox made incredible errors.

First, Jackson and center fielder Happy Felsch took off after a fly ball. Somehow, the ball landed between them. Meanwhile, the batter raced around first base.

Moving slowly, Felsch picked up the ball. He threw it to the second baseman—who missed the catch. The Reds soon scored their first run.

Three batters later, the Reds had only one out, and there were men on first and second. When a ball was hit deep into center field, Felsch went after it. He had caught hundreds of these kinds of balls before. Despite what happened earlier, surely this would be an easy out.

Felsch dropped the ball. In fact, he dropped it twice! Finally, he threw it to the shortstop, who then fired it home to the catcher.

Too late! The Reds scored another run.

As the game went on, the big bats of Chicago stayed silent. The game ended with a White Sox loss, 5–0.

Kid Gleason, the Chicago manager, told reporters, "Something is wrong. I don't know what it is."

Rumors swirled. Were the Sox losing on purpose? Were gamblers paying them to lose?

In game eight, in Chicago, Williams took the mound again. Fans still believed in him. They leaped to their feet, cheering him on.

Just fifteen pitches later, Williams had given up four hits and three runs. The Sox lost the game, 10–5, and the Series, five games to three.

One year later, eight Chicago players were accused of fixing the Series, and they were eventually banned from baseball forever. From then on the team became known as the Black Sox. Some confessed, including Jackson. Later, Jackson insisted he was innocent and didn't understand the accusation because he couldn't read or write.

Still, one story goes, a boy stopped Jackson outside the courtroom. "Say it ain't so, Joe," he pleaded. "Say it ain't so."

Without a word, Shoeless Joe just walked away.

“Shoeless” Joe Jackson (1881–1951)

Joseph Jefferson Jackson grew up in Greenville, South Carolina, the oldest of eight children. The family was poor. Jackson never went to school. By age six, he was working in cotton mills. Later on, he played for company baseball teams. Jackson got his nickname when he took off new, uncomfortable cleats, hit a triple, and was called a “shoeless son of a gun” by a fan of the other team. After baseball, Jackson owned a dry-cleaning business, a restaurant, and a liquor store.

Why would these players cheat?

Although they were the best team in baseball, the Sox were paid poorly. The team even charged players for cleaning their uniforms. (Actually, the team was called the Black Sox even before the fix, because of their dirty jerseys.)

These men had families, homes, and debt. Money was the reason why they cheated. But as Cicotte said later, "Now I've lost everything."

It was one of the lowest moments in baseball history.

World Series Winners

1910: Philadelphia Athletics over Chicago Cubs (Legendary manager Connie Mack took his team to the World Series four times in five years. He stayed with the team for fifty years.)

1911: Philadelphia Athletics over New York Giants

1912: Boston Red Sox over New York Giants (Game two is the only tie game in the history of the World Series; the game was called due to darkness.)

1913: Philadelphia Athletics over New York Giants

1914: Boston Braves over Philadelphia Athletics

1915: Boston Red Sox over Philadelphia Phillies

1916: Boston Red Sox over Brooklyn Robins

1917: Chicago White Sox over New York Giants

1918: Boston Red Sox over Chicago Cubs (After this Series, the Sox waited almost a century for another World Series championship.)

1919: Cincinnati Reds over Chicago White Sox

CHAPTER 4
1920s: New York at Bat

Many American homes had electricity now. More and more people drove cars. Life was easier, more fun. The Roaring Twenties were full of roaring good times.

In baseball, Babe Ruth was making big news. In 1921, he hit a record fifty-nine home runs in the regular season. That didn't help the Yankees in the World Series, though. They fell to the New York Giants that year and in 1922.

The Yankees and Giants met again in 1923, for the third straight year. Would the Bronx Bombers finally defeat their foes across the river?

In game one, it was 4–4 in the top of the ninth inning. Giant Casey Stengel was up to bat. He had a full count. He eyed the next pitch, then swung. He hit a line drive to center field. The ball rolled to the fence.

Stengel ran harder than he'd ever run before. He rounded first, then second. He stumbled. "I thought my shoe was coming off," he said later. But he kept running, his arms flying every which way. Gasping for breath, Stengel finally slid home. Safe! An inside-the-park home run! The final score—5–4, Giants.

But the next game, at the Giants home park, the Polo Grounds, Babe Ruth hit home runs in back-to-back at bats. The Yankees won 4–2.

What would happen in game three? The score was tied 0–0 through the seventh inning. Then, Casey Stengel came up to bat. He connected with a high fly that headed for the bleachers!

This time, Stengel took his time around the bases. He held up two fingers, for two homers. Then he thumbed his nose at the Yankee dugout. Rounding third, he blew the Yankees a kiss. It was the only run of the game—and it led to a win for the Giants.

Those hits, those games, made Stengel famous. Nevertheless, Babe Ruth and the Yankees took the Series and won their very first championship.

In 1927, the Yankees won again, with a lineup so deadly it was called "Murderers' Row." The Yankees swept the Series in 1928, too, with Ruth getting ten hits in just four games, with an unbelievable .625 batting average for the Series.

All three of his hits in game four were homers.

Ruth wasn't the only Yankee star. Another player homered in three of the four games. He was so threatening, Cardinal pitchers walked him five

times in a row. His name—Lou Gehrig. Where the Babe was loud and bigger than life, Gehrig was quiet and shy. Where the Babe made news off the field, driving fast cars and staying out all night, Gehrig

liked spending evenings at home with his wife.

But together, Ruth and Gehrig worked magic on the field.

In 1929, the mighty Yankees lost the pennant. It seemed the entire country was on a losing streak. The stock market crashed in October. People lost jobs and homes. It was the start of the Great Depression.

Lou Gehrig (1903–1941)

Gehrig was born in New York City. His family didn't have much money. His mom cleaned houses for a living. But she insisted Gehrig, an only child, go to college. Nicknamed the "Iron Horse," Gehrig played 2,130 straight games despite broken bones and back trouble—a record that lasted fifty-six years. He played for the Yankees his entire career.

In the 1928 Series, Gehrig had four homers, plus nine RBIs. He made the Cardinals so nervous that pitchers walked him in six plate appearances.

World Series Winners

1920: Cleveland Indians over Brooklyn Robins (Indian Elmer Smith hit the first World Series grand slam, while second baseman Bill Wasmsganss made an unassisted triple play—the first and only one so far.)

1921: New York Giants over New York Yankees (The first Series game broadcast on radio.)

1922: New York Giants over New York Yankees

1923: New York Yankees over New York Giants

1924: Washington Senators over New York Giants

1925: Pittsburgh Pirates over Washington Senators

1926: St. Louis Cardinals over New York Yankees

1927: New York Yankees over Pittsburgh Pirates

1928: New York Yankees over St. Louis Cardinals

1929: Philadelphia Athletics over Chicago Cubs

CHAPTER 5
1930s: Dynasty

The Depression hit almost every American. Millions were out of work. Breadlines, where people waited for free food, stretched for blocks.

But fans kept attending ball games. It was a way to forget their troubles.

And of course, there was still the Babe.

The 1932 Series saw one of baseball's legendary moments. That year, Babe Ruth and the Yankees faced the Chicago Cubs. They won two games in New York. For game three, they moved to Chicago, where angry Cubs fans threw fruit at Ruth. In answer, he hit a three-run homer in the first inning.

In the fifth, with the score tied, Ruth came up to bat again. Now some Cubs players yelled insults, too.

The Cubs pitcher threw a called strike. Ruth turned to the Cubs dugout and held up one finger. That was one strike. Two balls followed. Then came another called strike. Ruth held up two fingers. Two strikes. Was he taking the strikes on purpose?

Before the next pitch, Ruth seemed to point to center field, "calling his shot." That meant he was pointing where the ball would go.

The ball came toward Ruth. Ruth swung. The ball soared. It flew over the pitcher, over center field, into the bleachers for one of the longest hits

ever at Wrigley Field. People thought it went right where Babe had pointed!

Ruth circled the bases, clasping his hands over his head in victory.

Newspapers spread the story of the "called shot."

When asked if he called the home run, Ruth didn't really answer the question, saying, "It's in the papers. Isn't it?" Later, he admitted he held up the finger to show he had one strike left. "I never knew anybody who could tell you ahead of time where he was going to hit a baseball," he added.

Right after that famous hit, Lou Gehrig homered, too. The Yankees swept the Series. It would be Babe Ruth's last.

Lou Gehrig always played in Ruth's shadow. And now, with Ruth gone, another Yankee took the spotlight. In 1936, Joe DiMaggio teamed with Gehrig. He led the Yankees to four straight championship titles. The Yankees were a baseball dynasty.

Sadly, Gehrig's career ended in 1939. Early in the season, it was clear something was wrong; he couldn't hit, he couldn't field. The reason was that he had developed a rare muscle disease.

That summer, Gehrig was honored at Yankee Stadium. In his famous speech, thanking fans, he said, "Today I consider myself the luckiest man on the face of this earth." He died two years later, just

weeks before he would have turned thirty-eight.

Even without Gehrig, the Yankees ruled Depression-era America. They were appealing, clean-cut. DiMaggio seemed like a movie star.

Joe DiMaggio (1914–1999)

Giuseppe Paulo DiMaggio became another Yankee superstar. He grew up in San Francisco with four brothers and four sisters. Their father, a fisherman, wanted the boys to follow in his footsteps. But Joe had another idea—baseball—and so did his brothers Vince and Dominic. They played pro ball, too.

DiMaggio's fifty-six-game hitting streak for the Yankees made him a baseball star. But his style and grace off the field made him a celebrity. The great love of his life was actress Marilyn Monroe. And though they were divorced when she died, DiMaggio sent roses to her grave three times a week for twenty years.

But for one year, in 1934, a very different team took center stage: the St. Louis Cardinals.

Most of these men—like brothers Paul and Dizzy Dean—had grown up poor, without much education. They were a bunch of quarreling, messy oddballs who enjoyed practical jokes. Players threw water balloons from windows and pretended to fight in hotel lobbies.

The Gashouse Gang

1934 St. Louis Cardinals

The 1934 Cardinals were called the Gashouse Gang. Most likely the team was named for "gashouses," factories that turned coal into gas. These foul-smelling factories were in poor, rough neighborhoods. And maybe that's how the Cards saw themselves—poor and rough.

Still, the Cards made it to the World Series against the Detroit Tigers.

The Cards had fun—during one home game Dizzy played the tuba for fans. After three games, they were up two games to one.

Game four was in St. Louis. In the bottom of the fourth inning, the score was Detroit 4, St. Louis 3. But the Cards had men on first and third. In a surprise move, Dizzy came out to first base to pinch run. He bowed. Fans went crazy.

The next Card at bat hit a grounder. While Dizzy raced toward second, the Detroit second baseman tried for a double play. He threw the ball, which struck Dizzy hard—on the forehead. He fell to the ground, knocked out. The crowd fell silent.

Teammates carried Dizzy off the field. His brother Paul took him to the hospital. Later, Dizzy joked, "The doctors X-rayed my head and found nothing."

The Cards lost the game 10–4. After the two teams split games five and six, the clincher was held in Detroit. Fans packed into wooden bleachers built just for the Series.

With Dizzy back on the mound, the Cards were up 7–0 after six innings. Card Joe Medwick ran to third on a triple. He collided with Tiger Marv Owen. The two started to fight and had to be pulled apart.

Angry fans threw fruit, potatoes, anything they could find at Medwick. Attendants cleared the field. But it happened again and again. Finally, the baseball commissioner ordered Medwick to leave the game. It didn't hurt the Cards. They scored four more times for an 11–0 rout.

The few fans left had a pillow fight with seat pads. It was a fitting end to a World Series won by the Gashouse Gang.

World Series Winners

1930: Philadelphia Athletics over St. Louis Cardinals

1931: St. Louis Cardinals over Philadelphia Athletics

1932: New York Yankees over Chicago Cubs

1933: New York Giants over Washington Senators

1934: St. Louis Cardinals over Detroit Tigers

1935: Detroit Tigers over Chicago Cubs

1936 and 1937: New York Yankees over New York Giants

1938: New York Yankees over Chicago Cubs

1939: New York Yankees over Cincinnati Reds

CHAPTER 6
1940s: Color, Curses, and Dem Bums

By 1940 Europe was engaged in another world war. The US didn't enter the fighting until the very end of 1941, after the Yankees and the Dodgers had already faced off in the 1941 World Series.

The Dodgers were down two games to one, going into game four. The record-breaking temperature reached ninety-four degrees.

In the top of the ninth, the Dodgers led 4–3. Yankee batter Tommy Henrich had a full count with two outs.

The Dodgers were only one strike away from victory.

Henrich swung on the next pitch—and missed! That was it, everyone thought. The Dodgers had won! But catcher Mickey Owen dropped the ball.

When that happens on a third pitch, the batter can try to run. It was only Owen's fourth error of the entire season. But it was a big one. Henrich made it to first. And the Yankees wound up with a four-run rally.

"They'll never come back from this one," DiMaggio predicted. And he was right.

"Dem Bums"—the affectionate nickname Dodger fans gave their team—lost the game and the Series. The teams met again and again over the next fifteen years. And the Dodgers went down in defeat again and again—no matter how many times Brooklyn fans cried, "Wait till next year."

That next year, 1942, the US was in a full-out war with Japan, Germany, and their allies.

What would happen to baseball and the World Series?

The baseball commissioner asked President Roosevelt what he thought. Keep playing? Or stop, while Americans were fighting overseas? The president gave his answer in a famous letter: "I honestly feel that it would be best for the country to keep baseball going."

Still, more than five hundred Major League players served in the military, including stars Hank Greenberg of the Detroit Tigers, Ted Williams of the Red Sox, and "Joltin'" Joe DiMaggio of the Yankees.

In 1945, Greenberg came home to lead the Tigers to the pennant and a World Series contest against the Cubs.

President Franklin Roosevelt

Ted Williams

Game four of that Series, at Chicago's Wrigley Field, was the scene for one of the oddest moments in Series history. A fan arrived with two tickets, one for himself and one for his pet goat. When the goat was turned away, the man stormed off. According to legend, he said, "Cubs, they ain't gonna win no more."

The Cubs lost that game, then the Series. Was it the Curse of the Billy Goat?

Like the Cubs, the Red Sox were under a supposed curse, too: the Curse of the Bambino, named after the Babe.

In 1945, the war was over. And the next year, the Red Sox made it to the World Series for the first time since the team had sold Babe Ruth's contract. Would they be able to beat the Cardinals?

In the seventh-game clincher, the score was tied in the eighth. Cardinal Enos Slaughter was on first with two outs. The chances were good for a Boston victory. But the next batter blooped to short center field for what looked like a single.

The coach yelled at Slaughter to stop at third. Slaughter ignored him. He ran all the way home for the game-winning run. The Red Sox lost, and the "curse" continued.

The Dodgers continued losing to the Yankees, too, when the teams faced off in the World Series in 1947. Nevertheless, it was a historic season for the Dodgers—and for all of baseball.

Jackie Robinson had joined the Dodgers that year. He was the first African American to play on a Major League team.

It was a hard year for Robinson. Angry fans wrote letters threatening him and his family. From the stands, they called him ugly names. Opposing players taunted him, too, and dug cleats into his legs as he played first base. Still, Robinson helped Brooklyn capture the pennant. He helped pave the way for other black athletes, too. Now, about a third of all pro baseball players are men of color.

World Series Winners

1940: Cincinnati Reds over Detroit Tigers

1941: New York Yankees over Brooklyn Dodgers

1942: St. Louis Cardinals over New York Yankees

1943: New York Yankees over St. Louis Cardinals

1944: St. Louis Cardinals over St. Louis Browns

(The across-the-city teams shared one field.)

1945: Detroit Tigers over Chicago Cubs

1946: St. Louis Cardinals over Boston Red Sox

1947: New York Yankees over Brooklyn Dodgers

(first televised World Series)

1948: Cleveland Indians over Boston Braves

1949: New York Yankees over Brooklyn Dodgers

CHAPTER 7
1950s: The "Subway Series"

For most Americans, life was good in the 1950s. There were plenty of jobs. People bought homes and TVs. The first World Series game had been televised in 1947, on three local New York stations. But by the fifties, Series games were shown across the country. Airplane travel became common, too. Teams no longer took trains to games. They flew.

The Yankees even had their own plane. But they wouldn't need it for the 1951 Series against the Giants. It was a "Subway Series," meaning games were played between teams based in the same city—New York—so fans could travel to both stadiums by subway.

That year the "Oklahoma kid," Mickey Mantle, stepped onto center field. Only nineteen years old, he joined catcher Yogi Berra, pitching ace Whitey Ford, and Joe DiMaggio, who was playing in his last season and last World Series.

In game two, Giant Willie Mays—another rookie—hit a deep, high ball into center field. Mantle gave chase. But

he saw DiMaggio was taking it. Mantle stopped short. Somehow, his cleat caught on a drainpipe in the ground. He fell, wrenching his right knee. He was out for the rest of the Series.

Mickey's worried dad, Elvin "Mutt" Mantle, watched the accident from the Yankee dugout. Mutt managed to take Mickey to the hospital but collapsed on the sidewalk. He hadn't told his son he was sick—very sick. In fact, Mutt Mantle was dying.

After his father's death, Mickey Mantle played stronger than ever. His dad had been a huge baseball fan. Mickey was sure he was doing what his dad would have wanted.

In the next World Series, a Subway Series against the Dodgers, Mantle hit a double, a

triple, and two home runs. The Yankees had four championships in a row! The next year, they'd win again for a record five.

By now, the Dodgers had lost seven times to the Yankees. In 1955, the Dodgers thought maybe, just maybe, this would be their year. Jackie Robinson hoped so. At thirty-six, he was slowing down. He was still known for stealing bases, but he wasn't the runner he used to be.

In the eighth inning of game one, Jackie was on third base. He did his usual dance. Would he go for the steal? Pitcher Whitey Ford glanced at him. Then he started his windup.

Jackie took off. Just as Ford threw to catcher Yogi Berra, Robinson glided low into home plate. Safe! Jackie Robinson had stolen home in the World Series!

The Dodgers lost that game 6–5. But they won the championship, four games to three! Their first!

The next year, guess who was in the World Series. The Dodgers and the Yankees! The games were tied, two apiece. For game five, Yankee Don Larsen was on the mound.

Larsen had never been a star player. But on that day, batter after batter, inning after inning, he was perfect. After eight innings, the Dodgers didn't have a hit. The Yankees, meanwhile, had two runs. Now it was the top of the ninth. If Larsen retired the next three batters, he'd have a perfect game.

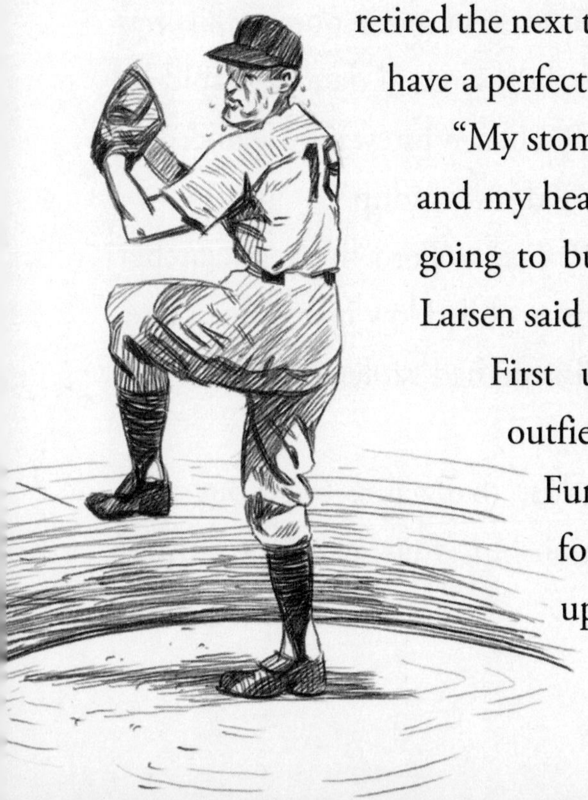

"My stomach was jumpin' and my head felt like it was going to burst wide open," Larsen said later.

First up was Dodger outfielder Carl Furillo. Furillo flied to right for an out. Second up was star catcher

Roy Campanella. He grounded to second for another out.

Larsen took off his cap and wiped his forehead.

Dale Mitchell came up to bat. Larsen threw the ball. One strike. Then two strikes. And three! Mitchell was out! Don Larsen had just pitched the first Series no-hitter. The first perfect game. And yet another Yankee championship.

In 1958, the Dodgers and Giants both left New York for California. There wouldn't be another Subway Series for forty-four years.

World Series Winners

1950: New York Yankees over Philadelphia Phillies

1951: New York Yankees over New York Giants

1952 and 1953: New York Yankees over Brooklyn Dodgers

1954: New York Giants over Cleveland Indians (Giant great Willie Mays made the play known everywhere as "The Catch"—a running over-the-shoulder grab right by the wall, which robbed Cleveland of a hit and a run.)

1955: Brooklyn Dodgers over New York Yankees

1956: New York Yankees over Brooklyn Dodgers

1957: Milwaukee Braves over New York Yankees ("Hammering" Hank Aaron, who'd go on to break the career home run record, led the Braves with three homers and nine RBIs.)

1958: New York Yankees over Milwaukee Braves

1959: Los Angeles Dodgers over Chicago White Sox

CHAPTER 8
1960s: Maz, and a Miracle

The sixties were a decade of change—change in music, fashion, politics. Major League baseball was changing, too. By the end of the decade, each league grew to twelve teams. There were ball clubs in San Diego, Seattle, Minneapolis, Atlanta, and even Canada.

The Yankees opened the decade with a bang. The "M and M Boys," Mickey Mantle and MVP slugger Roger Maris, faced the Pittsburgh Pirates in the 1960 World Series. Pirates star Roberto Clemente was the first Latino Major Leaguer.

Roberto Clemente

It was a close seventh game, filled with errors and home runs. In the bottom of the ninth, Pittsburgh came to the plate. The score was tied at nine. And the pressure was on for lead-off batter, Bill "Maz" Mazeroski. The second baseman was a brilliant fielder. Nicknamed "No Hands," he caught and threw so quickly, his hands were a blur. But Mazeroski was never strong at bat.

Mazeroski swung on the second pitch. He connected. And the ball soared over the left field wall. Game and Series over. Maz skipped around the bases.

The Yankees, however, weren't down for long. They won the next two Series. The LA Dodgers took two titles also, helped by lefty pitcher Sandy Koufax.

Sandy Koufax (born December 30, 1935)

Sanford "Sandy" Koufax grew up in Brooklyn, New York, and played for the Dodgers—in Brooklyn and LA—his entire career. As their number one pitcher, Koufax was expected to pitch the World Series opener in 1965. He didn't. The game fell on Yom Kippur, the holiest Jewish holiday. Koufax is Jewish. And while he didn't usually attend religious services, he felt it was important to observe the day. Koufax went on to pitch games two, five, and seven. Helping his team to victory, he was named Series MVP.

But the biggest Series story of the decade happened in 1969.

The New York Mets joined the NL in 1962. They lost 120 games their first season. In fact, they finished at the bottom of the league every year. But something happened in 1969. That summer, astronaut Neil Armstrong walked on the moon. People joked that even that wasn't as amazing as the Mets. They made it to the World Series.

The Amazin' Mets faced the Orioles. Baltimore was considered one of the strongest teams—ever. But their power hitters, Boog Powell, Frank Robinson, and Brooks Robinson, couldn't knock in runs. By the fifth game, the Mets were up three games to one. They could clinch the title.

But in the seventh inning, they were down by a run.

Al Weis came up to bat. He'd homered twice the entire season. Now, he blasted a hit into the left field stands to tie the game.

The Miracle Mets scored two more times to win. It was one of the biggest upsets in World Series history. An "amazin'" way to end the decade.

World Series Winners

1960: Pittsburgh Pirates over New York Yankees

1961: New York Yankees over Cincinnati Reds

1962: New York Yankees over San Francisco Giants

1963: Los Angeles Dodgers over New York Yankees

1964: St. Louis Cardinals over New York Yankees

1965: Los Angeles Dodgers over Minnesota Twins

1966: Baltimore Orioles over Los Angeles Dodgers

1967: St. Louis Cardinals over Boston Red Sox

1968: Detroit Tigers over St. Louis Cardinals

1969: New York Mets over Baltimore Orioles

An official baseball program featuring the 1869 Cincinnati Red Stockings

National Baseball Hall of Fame Library/Getty Images

Baseball's first professional team—the Cincinnati Red Stockings

National Baseball Hall of Fame Library/Getty Images

The Huntington Avenue Grounds in Boston, Massachusetts, 1903

© Bertmann/CORBIS

The eight Chicago "Black Sox" players in court, 1919

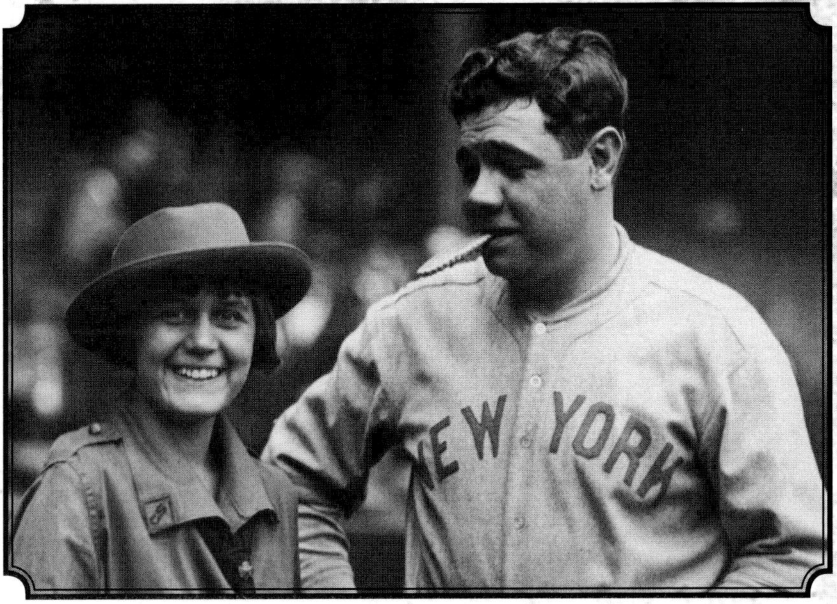

© Underwood & Underwood/Corbis

Babe Ruth poses with a Girl Scout, 1923

Lou Gehrig at bat in Yankee Stadium, 1920s

Joe DiMaggio homers during his first at bat in the 1936 World Series

President Franklin Delano Roosevelt throws the first pitch at Fenway Park in Boston, 1938

Babe Ruth puts an arm around Lou Gehrig after Gehrig's farewell speech, 1939

St. Louis Cardinals' Enos Slaughter slides into home plate, 1946

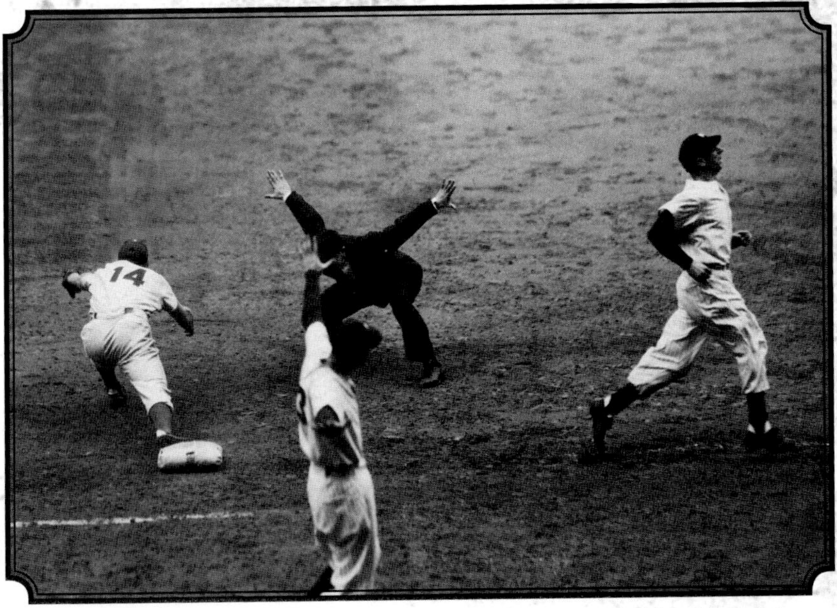

Joe DiMaggio is safe at first during the subway series in New York, 1947

The 1952 Brooklyn Dodgers rush the field during practice

"The Catch"—Willie Mays makes an over-the-shoulder catch during Game 1 of the 1954 World Series in New York

Milwaukee Braves catcher Del Crandall leaps over
Willie Mays as he slides safely home, 1959

ASSOCIATED PRESS

Fans rush the field after Bill Mazeroski hits a series-winning home run for the Pittsburgh Pirates, 1960

USHER

The Pittsburgh Pirates' Roberto Clemente bats
against the Baltimore Orioles, 1971

Neil Leifer/Getty Images

The 1976 Cincinnati Reds and New York Yankees
line up on the field before Game 1 in Cincinnati

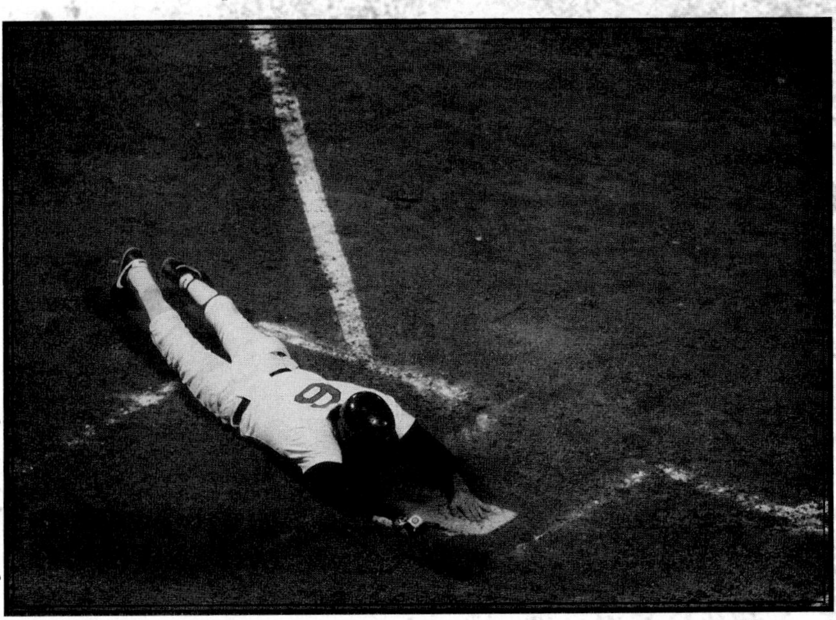

George Tiedemann/Getty Images

Boston Red Sox' Bill Buckner is safe at home during the 1986 World Series

John Iacono/Getty Images

Giants player Kelly Downs carries his nephew after an earthquake hits Candlestick Park in San Francisco, 1989

Richard Mackson/Getty Images

Atlanta Braves catcher Greg Olson flips on his head after tagging out the Minnesota Twins' Dan Gladden, 1991

MLB Photos/Getty Images

Twins' Kirby Puckett at bat in Minnesota, 1994

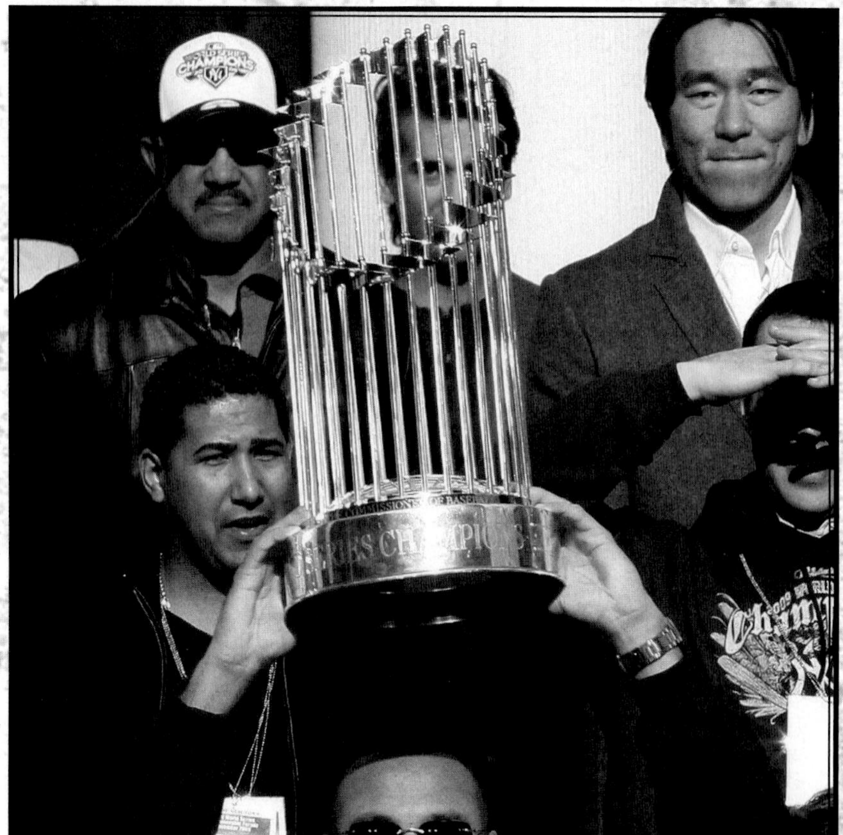

Jim McIsaac/Getty Images

Yankees' Derek Jeter holds the World Series trophy during a victory parade in New York, 2009

CHAPTER 9
1970s: Still Cursed

The Oakland Athletics, Cincinnati Reds—and, of course, the Yankees—dominated the seventies. And right smack in the middle of the decade? There was a standout Series.

The 1975 NL winners—the Reds, who starred Pete Rose, Ken Griffey, and Johnny Bench.

Pete Rose Kenn Griffey Johnny Bench

The 1975 AL winners—the Boston Red Sox, led by veterans Carl Yastrzemski and Luis Tiant.

The Reds, known as the Big Red Machine, were favored to win. They were clean-shaven and all business. The Sox were scrappy, scruffy, and underdogs.

The teams traded wins. Game six was one of the most exciting in World Series history.

It was held at night, a home game for Boston. They needed the win to stay alive. In the eighth inning, the Reds had a 6–3 lead. Boston, at bat, already had two outs. Pinch hitter Bernie Carbo stepped up to the plate. He'd always struggled to stay in the lineup. But, with the pressure on, he hit a three-run homer.

At the end of the ninth inning, the score was tied 6–6.

It was past midnight when the bottom of the twelfth began.

Sox catcher Carlton Fisk waited in the batter's box. In came a low sinker. Fisk swung.

The ball rose high in the air. It floated along the left field line. Was it in foul territory or not? Fisk wasn't sure. He danced a few steps toward first. He waved his arms, as if he could push the ball fair. Finally, the ball struck high on the foul pole netting. A homer! A game winner! Boston celebrated the moment. The Sox, still "cursed," lost the clincher and the Series.

The 1976 Reds, with its "8 Great" starting lineup, beat the Yankees. But the next year, the Yankees were in the Series again, this time against the LA Dodgers.

Reggie Jackson had joined New York that season. Some teammates thought Jackson was all talk. That he didn't work hard enough on the field that year.

But in the 1977 Series, he scored big in the first five games. The Yanks were up three games to two.

During batting practice before game six, Jackson cleared the wall of Yankee Stadium almost every time. Fans gave him a standing ovation. But they hadn't seen anything yet.

In the bottom of the fourth, Jackson swung on his very first pitch. He ripped it into the right field stands for a two-run homer. In the bottom of the fifth, he blasted the first pitch again, for another two-run homer. In the bottom of the eighth, he hit the first pitch once more, sending it into the center-field bleachers. Three times in a row, Jackson hit his first pitch over the wall.

Jackson tied Babe Ruth's record for home runs in a World Series game, and set a new one: five home runs in one World Series. No wonder he's called Mr. October.

World Series Winners

1970: Baltimore Orioles over Cincinnati Reds

1971: Pittsburgh Pirates over Baltimore Orioles (Game four was first Series game held at night.)

1972: Oakland Athletics over Cincinnati Reds

1973: Oakland Athletics over New York Mets

1974: Oakland Athletics over Los Angeles Dodgers (The A's became three-peat winners!)

1975: Cincinnati Reds over Boston Red Sox

1976: Cincinnati Reds over New York Yankees (First Series to use designated hitters)

1977: New York Yankees over Los Angeles Dodgers

1978: New York Yankees over Los Angeles Dodgers

1979: Pittsburgh Pirates over Baltimore Orioles (Throughout the year, Pirate leader Willie Stargell handed out "Stargell Stars" to teammates for good work. He guided them to a Series win, clinching the seventh game with a homer.)

CHAPTER 10
1980s: An Error and an Earthquake

In the eighties, most ball clubs were in the running for the pennant. Would this be the decade the Red Sox finally broke their "curse"?

In 1986, they faced the Mets.

The Red Sox were ahead three games to two, when the Series moved to Shea Stadium in Queens, New York. But every time Boston pulled ahead in game six, New York tied it up.

By the top of the tenth inning, the Sox took the field. They still felt confident. They were three outs away from the championship. The scoreboard flashed, "Congratulations, Red Sox."

First baseman Bill Buckner had a bad sprain. In every Series game they'd won, the manager had taken him out toward the end. But now Buckner stayed in. What could be the harm?

Two batters up, two batters down. The Sox were one out away from victory. But the next three batters singled, and one run came in. The score—Red Sox still up 5–4.

Met Mookie Wilson stepped up to the plate. The count went to two balls and two strikes. Then came a wild pitch. The runner on third raced home. And the score was tied.

Wilson swung at the next pitch. The ball bounced toward first. It seemed like it would be an easy out. But somehow, the ball rolled through Buckner's legs. Wilson was safe on first, and another Met scored. New York won the game, plus the Series in game seven.

Boston fans forgave Buckner. After all, it wasn't his fault. The "curse" had struck again.

The next year, it was an all-California Series. The A's faced the team across the Bay Bridge, the San Francisco Giants. The favored A's took the first two games in Oakland, thanks to the big bats of Jose Canseco and Mark McGwire.

On Tuesday evening, October 17, the Series moved to Candlestick Park.

The night was warm and still, unusual for San Francisco. By five o'clock, sixty-two thousand fans were at the park. Players waited on the field to be announced.

At 5:04 p.m., a roar swept through the stands. The ground shook. Walls, seats, everything shifted. It was an earthquake!

Police ordered everyone to leave. Players rushed from the field to find their

families. Fans hurried to the exits.

Outside, the entire city was blacked out. The Bay Bridge was cracked. Sixty-three people died. Three thousand were injured. And thousands more lost their homes. But everyone in Candlestick made it out safely.

The Series was postponed for ten days. In the end, the A's swept the Giants, just as everyone expected. But no one could have predicted the earthquake. The World Series is never a sure thing!

World Series Winners

1980: Philadelphia Phillies over Kansas City Royals

1981: Los Angeles Dodgers over New York Yankees

1982: St. Louis Cardinals over Milwaukee Brewers

1983: Baltimore Orioles over Philadelphia Phillies

1984: Detroit Tigers over San Diego Padres

1985: Kansas City Royals over St. Louis Cardinals (A bad call—that the ump later admitted was a mistake—gave the Royals a runner at first, changing the game and the Series.)

1986: New York Mets over Boston Red Sox

1987: Minnesota Twins over St. Louis Cardinals

1988: Los Angeles Dodgers over Oakland Athletics (An injured Kirk Gibson had one at bat in the entire Series—hitting a two-out, two-run homer in the ninth inning of game one, to win the game and inspire his teammates.)

1989: Oakland Athletics over San Francisco Giants

CHAPTER 11
1990s: Worst to First

The century closed with surprising winners and losers. In 1991, both league champions went from worst to first. The Atlanta Braves played the Minnesota Twins in one of the tightest Series on record. In fact, four games came down to the last at bat.

After game five, the Braves were up three games to two. Before the next game, Kirby Puckett made an announcement in the clubhouse: "You guys should jump on my back tonight. I'm going to carry us."

In the first inning, Puckett tripled in a run. In the third inning, playing the field, the five-foot-eight Puckett scaled the fence for a leaping catch to save a home run. Still, the game went into extra innings.

In the eleventh, Puckett came up to bat. Fans screamed, "Kirby! Kirby!" On a two-and-one count, he slammed the ball over the left-center fence. The Twins won "The Puckett Game" and the clincher.

That game-winning pitcher, Jack Morris, went on to play for the Toronto Blue Jays. In 1992, they became the first team outside the United States to win the World Series. Then they did it again in 1993. Would they three-peat in 1994?

No. The players went on strike. They were protesting against a salary cap, a limit on the money a team could pay its athletes. They stopped playing, and the season ended in August. For the first time since 1905, there was no World Series.

In 1995, the Fall Classic was back. But where were the Yankees? They hadn't won a World Series in sixteen years. And they hadn't put in an appearance since 1981.

The team had been trying to improve. And in 1996, they finally took the title once again. In fact, the Yankees won the next three out of four Series, thanks to superstar Derek Jeter, ace reliever Mariano Rivera, and a host of solid batters and pitchers. Would they be a new dynasty for the new century?

Mariano Rivera

World Series Winners

1990: Cincinnati Reds over Oakland Athletics

1991: Minnesota Twins over Atlanta Braves

1992: Toronto Blue Jays over Atlanta Braves

1993: Toronto Blue Jays over Philadelphia Phillies

1994: No World Series

1995: Atlanta Braves over Cleveland Indians

1996: New York Yankees over Atlanta Braves

1997: Florida Marlins over Cleveland Indians (The first wild card team to reach the Series, clinched the title with a hit by Edgar Renteria.)

1998: New York Yankees over San Diego Padres

1999: New York Yankees over Atlanta Braves

CHAPTER 12
2000s: Standing Together

On September 11, 2001, terrorists in hijacked planes attacked New York City and Washington, DC. Nearly three thousand people died. The country was shaken to its core.

One month later, the Yankees were in the World Series. Yankee Stadium was just nine miles from the crash site. For the first New York game, security had to be tight. Nearby air traffic was banned. More than a thousand police officers stood guard.

Emotions ran high. The tattered flag from the World Trade Center waved. Fans waved their own flags, chanting, “USA! USA!”

The Yankees were hoping to win their fourth title in a row. That had happened only two times before in baseball history, and both times by Yankees teams.

The Arizona Diamondbacks, in their first Series appearance, wanted to stop them. In games one and two, at their home field, they did. But the Yankees took the next three, in front of cheering New York crowds.

The deciding games were back in Arizona. In the eighth inning of game seven, the Yankees were up 2–1.

In came Yankee top reliever Mariano Rivera. He’d never—ever—lost a postseason game. Sure enough, Rivera struck out all three Arizona batters.

But in the ninth, with Arizona runners on first and second, Tony Womack doubled. One man came home, and the score stood 2–2.

Shockingly, Rivera hit the next batter. The bases were loaded.

Up stepped batter Luis Gonzales. He knew he had to get the ball into play. So he swung and sent a blooper over Derek Jeter's head. It was a single, the game, and the Series.

The Yankees lost to the Florida Marlins in 2003. Another surprise. Then, in the 2004 AL

Championship playoffs, they faced the Red Sox, their biggest rivals.

Boston was down three games to none. But they came back to take the Series, with Curt Schilling pitching on an injured ankle. One game, his sock was even soaked with blood. With that kind of energy, the Sox couldn't lose. They swept the Cardinals in the Series.

The Curse of the Bambino was finally broken!

In 2007 the Sox swept the Colorado Rockies for another World Series championship. And in 2013 they had yet another chance to take the title. Nobody expected much of the team. The year before, they ended the season in last place. They'd lost their manager and some key players. But tragedy brought the team together.

On April 15, the Red Sox played at Fenway Park in the morning. It was the same day as the famed Boston Marathon—a 26.2-mile race. At 2:49 p.m., a bomb exploded near the race's finish line. Three people died. More than one hundred people were seriously injured. It was another act of terror. And it left a city in horror.

The Sox visited the Marathon victims throughout the season. Before every game, they hung up a jersey with the words "Boston Strong" in the dugout. The players bonded by shaving their heads and growing beards. They kept the look through the season, the playoffs, and the World Series—once again against the Cards.

In the first five games, designated hitter David Ortiz went eleven for fifteen. In the sixth game, Cardinal pitchers walked him four times. But Boston still clinched the Series.

Two million people lined Boston streets for the victory parade. The Red Sox set the trophy on the Marathon finish line to honor the victims, the runners, and the city.

Once again, the World Series proved to be more than a sports contest. Through the decades, through the centuries, the Series has become part of American history.

FINISH

In 2016, the championship games linked *two* centuries to make history. The Chicago Cubs faced the Cleveland Indians. Both teams had gone longer than any others in the Major League without a World Series title. The Cubs, hoping to break the Curse of the Billy Goat, had been waiting over a hundred years.

The Cubs won 103 games in the regular season. Just four years earlier, they had 101 losses. Now, in the postseason, after four games the series stood at Indians 3, Cubs 1. The Indians needed just one more win to grab the championship.

Then the Cubs won Game 5, at home. Now they traveled to Cleveland. The odds still seemed against them. But they wound up on top again. So it all came down to Game 7.

Everyone across the country knew about Chicago and the famous curse. This could make history.

At first, it looked like a Cubs victory. They had five runs in the first five innings. Going into the eighth, the Cubs held the lead, 6–3. But the Indians scored again and again for a tie ball game. It stayed tied in the ninth, with the Indians still sweeping up the momentum.

Now the weather joined the drama. It began to pour. A rain delay was called.

Cubs outfielder Jason Heyward herded all twenty-five teammates into a tiny weight room. Usually a quiet player, Heyward surprised everyone with a speech. He wanted his teammates to know he was proud of them. That he loved them. That they were the best team in baseball.

It sparked the team. They were ready for anything. First at bat: Kyle Schwarber. He'd been out all season with a knee injury. But now he singled! The next batter drew a walk. Then Ben Zobrist stepped up to the plate. He delivered an RBI double! After another walk, Miguel Montero singled, and a runner came home.

At the bottom of the tenth, the Cubs were up by two. The Indians weren't about to give up. With two outs, they scored a run. The next batter hit a slow grounder. Third baseman Kris Bryant scooped up the ball. Grinning, he threw to first. The stadium fell silent. When Anthony Rizzo caught the ball and stepped on the bag for the out, Cubs fans screamed with joy. Finally, after such a long time, they'd won the World Series.

The 2017 World Series again brought the

trophy to a city that had recently experienced very hard times. Two months after Hurricane Harvey devastated the Houston area with more than three feet of rain, the Houston Astros won the World Series over the LA Dodgers—the first in the team's fifty-five-year history!

The Series was a seven-game thriller that broke many records, including most home runs in a single World Series game (eight) and most total home runs across a World Series tournament (twenty-five).

The Dodgers had another shot at winning the Series when they faced the Boston Red Sox in 2018. They lost to Boston five games to one. But a new record was set for longest World Series game in history: Game 3 lasted for seven hours and twenty minutes!

So will any records be broken in the next World Series? Will there be plays that go down in sports history? You'll have to keep watching to find out!

World Series Winners

2000: New York Yankees over New York Mets

2001: Arizona Diamondbacks over New York Yankees

2002: Anaheim Angels over San Francisco Giants

2003: Florida Marlins over New York Yankees

2004: Boston Red Sox over St. Louis Cardinals

2005: Chicago White Sox over Houston Astros

2006: St. Louis Cardinals over Detroit Tigers

2007: Boston Red Sox over Colorado Rockies

2008: Philadelphia Phillies over Tampa Bay Rays

2009: New York Yankees over Philadelphia Phillies

2010: San Francisco Giants over Texas Rangers

2011: St. Louis Cardinals over Texas Rangers

2012: San Francisco Giants over Detroit Tigers

2013: Boston Red Sox over St. Louis Cardinals

2014: San Francisco Giants over Kansas City Royals

2015: Kansas City Royals over New York Mets

2016: Chicago Cubs over Cleveland Indians

2017: Houston Astros over Los Angeles Dodgers

2018: Boston Red Sox over Los Angeles Dodgers

2019: Washington Nationals over Houston Astros

Timeline of World Series

1876	National League founded on February 2
1882	Pennant winners Cincinnati Reds (National League) and Chicago White Sox (American Association) play the first postseason series
1901	American League founded on January 28
1903	First modern World Series between AL's Boston team and NL's Pittsburgh team
1908	Second Series win for Chicago Cubs
1919	Black Sox scandal
1921	First Subway Series, Giants over Yankees
	First Series to be broadcast on radio
1927	Yankees' Murderers' Row lineup, including Babe Ruth and Lou Gehrig, sweeps the Series
1934	St. Louis Cardinals, called the Gashouse Gang, take the World Series
1947	First televised World Series, Yankees vs. Dodgers
	First Major League black player, Jackie Robinson, plays in the Series
1955	The Brooklyn Dodgers win their first Series, finally defeating archrival Yankees
1969	The Miracle Mets beat the Orioles in a historic upset
1977	Reggie Jackson hits three homers in a row, all on first pitches, to lead the Yankees to victory
1989	World Series interrupted by a San Francisco earthquake
2004	Eighty-six years after winning their last championship, the Red Sox win a Series
2016	One hundred eight years after winning their last championship, the Cubs win a Series

Timeline of the World

1876	Alexander Graham Bell is granted the patent for the first telephone
1882	Circus owner P. T. Barnum buys Jumbo, the famous elephant
1901	The twenty-fifth US president, William McKinley, is assassinated by Leon Czolgosz
1903	The Wright brothers make the first airplane flight
1908	Mother's Day is first observed
1920	The Nineteenth Amendment to the US Constitution gives women the right to vote
1929	The New York stock market crashes in October, leading to the Great Depression
1933	Adolf Hitler takes power in Germany
1945	World War II ends
1955	The board game Scrabble is sold in stores
1969	Astronaut Neil Armstrong walks on the moon
	Woodstock music festival is held in Upstate New York
1976	Apple Computer, Inc. is founded by Stephen Wozniak and Steven Jobs
1986	Five million people hold hands from California to New York for "Hands Across America" to fight hunger and poverty
1989	An Exxon oil tanker, the *Valdez*, spills eleven million gallons of oil off the coast of Alaska
2004	Social network Facebook launches at Harvard University
2016	Activist and boxing great Muhammad Ali dies at seventy-four

Bibliography

***Books for young readers**

Abrams, Roger, I. ***The First World Series and the Baseball Fanatics of 1903***. Boston: Northeastern University Press, 2003.

Asinof, Eliot. ***Eight Men Out: The Black Sox and the 1919 World Series***. New York: Henry Holt and Company, 1963.

* Buckley, James, Jr. ***World Series***. New York: DK Publishing, 2004

* Christopher, Matt, with text by Stephanie Peters. ***The World Series: The Greatest Moments of the Most Exciting Games***. New York: Little Brown and Company, 2007.

Fimrite, Ron. ***Sports Illustrated: The World Series: A History of Baseball's Fall Classic***. New York: Time Inc. Home Entertainment, 1997.

Heidenry, John. ***The Gashouse Gang***. New York: Public Affairs, 2007.

Leventhal, Josh. ***The World Series: An Illustrated Encyclopedia of the Fall Classic***. New York: Black Dog and Leventhal Publishers, 2001.

Website

www.thisgreatgame.com. This Great Game: The Online Book of Baseball History.